El Héroe

Translation Copyright © M. San Pedro 2024
All rights reserved

ISBN 978-1-945028-62-5 (hardcover)
ISBN 978-1-945028-64-9 (paperback)

First published by St. Vitus Dance

Book design and production assistance by Adam Robinson for Good Book Developers (goodbookdevelopers.com)

Editing by Savannah Crenshaw (linktr.ee/savannahcrenshaw)

Please visit https://StVitus.Dance

"The one who lords over himself will lord over everyone."

—King Fernando the Catholic, King of Aragón

El Héroe

The Valiant Hero (1637)

Baltasar Gracián

Translated by M. San Pedro

Contents

Preliminary Note — ix
About this Book — x
To Don Juan Bautista Brescia — xii
To the Lecturers — xiii

I   The Hero: Armed with Virtue and Cloaked in Incomprehensibility — 1
II   Concealer of Intentions — 4
III   Ingenuity: The Hero's Greatest Strength — 7
IV   The Heart of a King — 11
V   A Man of Relevant Taste — 14
VI   A Man of Eminence — 18
VII   The Excellence of Being First — 22
VIII   May the Hero Prefer Reasonable Endeavors — 25
IX   The Most Precious Diamond — 28
X   May the Hero Test His Fortune Before Committing Himself — 31
XI   May the Hero Know When to Retire, with Fortune at His Side — 35
XII   Winning the Grace of Others — 39
XIII   The Natural Hero — 42
XIV   Born to Command — 45
XV   A Hero of Sublime Sympathy — 48
XVI   Greatness Renewed — 51
XVII   Every Gift Without Affectation — 54
XVIII   If You Wish to Be Great, You Must Emulate Greatness — 56
XIX   A Critical Paradox — 59
XX   The Greatest Crown Jewel and the Phoenix of a Hero's Gifts — 61

Works by Baltasar Gracián — 67
About the Translator — 69

Preliminary Note

I, M. San Pedro, present a modernized English translation of *El Héroe: The Valiant Hero (1637)* by Lorenzo Gracián[1] of Huesca, Spain. In order to facilitate the reading of the text for the non-specialized public, I chose to offer a modernized edition allowing for further clarification of Gracián's *conceptismo* style of writing and, when I considered it appropriate, issued amendments to the text in order to make it easier to comprehend in contemporary times. These amendments are few and seldom, only occurring where I felt that further clarification was needed for the benefit of the reader. It was of the utmost importance to me that I present a version that preserves the integrity of the original writing, even in its punctuation and spacing. I am more than certain that this modern English translation will be found insightful, lucid, digestible, and, most importantly, effective.

---

1   Lorenzo Gracián is the pseudonym under which Baltasar Gracián first began publishing. Only his closest friends, Dr. Juan Francisco Andrés, Don Vincencio Juan de Lastanosa, Dr. Juan Orencio de Lastanosa, and Dr. Don Manuel de Salinas y Lizana, knew of his real identity.

About this Book

El Héroe: The Valiant Hero (1637) by Baltasar Gracián is an instructive manual that provides the reader with twenty primary qualities that any leader or ruler should possess in order to achieve perfection. Father Gracián's intention, as he mentions in the book, is to offer an "oracle to guide you towards excellence" and "towards the art of being illustrious" so that men can know how to successfully face the challenges of their epoch and do so in a manner that is compatible with the Christian faith and doctrine.

In this treatise, he powerfully constructs the ideal type of Christian knight and manages in just twenty short but dense chapters to unbosom the definition of singularity and perfection in a leader, using as examples the lives of Roman emperors, the kings of Aragón, the Spanish kings of the House of Austria, and the kings of France, as well as warriors, diplomats, and the courtiers linked to them.

El Héroe is a work of profane subject matter. Despite his deep respect for religion, it was published without the approval of the church, which meant significant problems for Father Gracián, since his Jesuit superiors considered it a book that was not compatible with his status as a priest nor with the Catholic faith. And, in spite of trying to protect himself by signing his works with the name of his brother "Lorenzo" or with the pseudonym "García de Marlones," he would carry this burden for the rest of his life. The persecution within his order reached a tipping point in 1658 when he was publicly reprimanded, put on a diet of bread and water, and dismissed from his chair in Zaragoza. This persecution would significantly impact his health and ultimately cost him his life later that same year.

El Padre, as I affectionately refer to him, is considered the great precursor of modern thought, and with *El Héroe,* as with the rest of his works, he manages to put together a very complete compendium of the material means available to a man for him to achieve perfection and success in a pessimistic and somewhat fatalistic society; that expects more solutions of divine origin than fruit of human work, dedication, and ambition.

Gracián struggled until the end of his life to improve the men of his time. His works are a wealth of advice, warnings, and rules for anyone who wishes to flee from the mediocrity that, according to him, abounds, not only in the Spanish kingdoms but also in the entire world.

El Héroe is the first of his seven masterpieces, and it is the result of his conscientious study for more than fifteen years of the thoughts and experiences of Emperors Alexander and Julius Caesar, the kings of Spain—Don Juan II, Fernando the Catholic, Philip II, Philip IV, the Holy Roman Emperor Charles V, and many of their select ministers and captains— as well as Seneca, Aesop, Homer, Aristotle, and Baldassare Castiglione, the Count of Casatico, among others; and in its twenty chapters, we find all of this knowledge and work condensed. With this masterpiece, he offers us a compact collection of advice that, despite being almost four centuries old, is still extraordinarily relevant and useful in guiding men towards excellence.

The spirit of Father Gracián lives through the pages of this book. Allow his wisdom and instruction to shape you into a Superior Man and a Valiant Hero.

—M. San Pedro

To Don Juan Bautista Brescia

Apostolic Prothonotary and Doctor of Both Rights

El Héroe: The Valiant Hero, like a child, runs towards the arms that I consider open in your mercy to receive him. If it is my destiny, I joyfully confess my obligation and debt through him; and, if it is your inclination, may the good nature that the author of him has communicated to him be discovered. And, while he is well adorned with so many charms of virtue, he cannot live in harmony until Your Grace, with the ultimate hand and the last say, calls him perfect. As a Hero, he requests the illustrious patronage of Don Brescia. As an apprentice of prudence, he intends to be instructed by the masters of antiquity. And, in order to become accomplished in all faculty and science, he dedicates himself to applying the doctrines that Your Grace teaches: showing much promise by threatening to be great, which is the main component of being a King. El Héroe, The Valiant Hero, hopes to secure Your Grace's affection with the performance of my offer.

—Pedro de Quesada

To the Lecturers

How singular I wish you to become! I undertake to form with this small book a great man who, with brief intervals, performs immortal deeds. To bring out of you a maximum male, that is a miracle of perfection, and although you are not by nature a king, you may carry yourself like one through the advantages of virtue.

Virtue formed the prudent Seneca; the sagacious Aesop; the warlike Homer; Aristotle, the philosopher; Tacitus, the politician; and the great courtier, Baldassare Castiglione, Count of Casatico.

I, by copying some of the virtues of these great masters, intend to remake you into a Hero and a universal prodigy. For this, I wrote this treatise, a manual of other people's wisdom and my own mistakes. Perhaps it will flatter you or warn you, and perhaps in it you will see either what you already are or what you should be.

Here you have not a political or economic discourse but a discourse on reason and on the art of governing yourself—an oracle to guide you towards excellence and towards the art of being illustrious with few rules of discretion. I write briefly, for your understanding is plentiful, and short, for my thinking is limited.

I do not want to detain you any longer; go forward and become the man that Heaven has destined you to be.

Rodrigo Díaz de Vivar, known as *"El Cid"* (the Lord and Master), was a Castilian mercenary, knight, devoted husband, father, and ruler of the kingdom of Valencia. Considered the greatest of all medieval knights, he was undefeated in battle and is still today Spain's celebrated national hero, representing the ideal masculine man: intelligent, strong, valiant, loyal, just, and pious.

-I-

The Hero: Armed with Virtue and Cloaked in Incomprehensibility

This is the first skill in the art of connoisseuring: to engage circumstances with ingenuity. It is a great trick to show off your knowledge but not be comprehended; to prime with expectations, satisfy, but still leave desire. Promising and fulfilling much, but still leaving greater hopes for the future.

(1) Let the cultured Hero probe the bottom of his heart if he wants to be venerated by all. A river is formidable until a ford is found, and a man is only respected until his capacity is known. And so, it is far better to remain mysterious—of presumed depth—and maintain reverence through suspicion.

(2) To discover is to master; concealing yourself allows you to alternate victory between subjects. The one who comprehends all is Lord over all, and the one who cloaks himself in mystery never needs to yield.

(3) The dexterity of the wise man in concealing himself competes with the curiosity of the attentive ones trying to know him, and he instantly recognizes the beginnings of their attempts.

(4) The wise man never reveals the extent of his strengths all at once. He slowly advances, revealing a little at a time, to the delight of those around him and to the surprise of his enemies. His advantage is being an infinite entity, or, at least, appearing to be so.

This is the first rule of greatness: if not to be infinite, to seem so, which is no easy subtlety. Those with scruples will applaud the crude paradox of the Greek Sage Pittacus of Mytilene: "The half is greater than the whole, because half on display and the other in reserve are more than an entire whole fully within view."

(5) King Fernando the Catholic was a master of incomprehensibility and all other skills; he was the great first king of the New World, the last one of Aragón, and the *ne plus ultra*[2] of all heroic kings.

He ruled over his Catholic monarchy, always attentive, and competed against other kings, holding them in suspense—more with the virtues of his spirit, which every day shone brighter, than with the new crowns of the kingdoms he acquired.

(6) But the one who was dazzled by this center of the rays of prudence, the great restorer of the Gothic monarchy, was his heroic queen, Queen Isabella, and after her, the nobles and knights of the palace, who probed his mind, attempted to scan his depths, and were eager to measure his value.

But how masterfully King Fernando circumvented them—sometimes allowing them and at other times stopping them—how cautiously he granted them and denied them! And, at last, he won them.

---

2   *Ne plus ultra:* Latin phrase meaning "no more beyond."

(7) Oh, candidate of fame! Thou who aspires to greatness, be alert to primness and devoted to excellence. Let all know thee and let none embrace thee; for by this ruse, what is moderate will seem like much, what is much will seem infinite, and what is infinite, even more.

-II-

Concealer of Intentions

(1) Mastering this great art would be insufficient if it only dictated showing restraint in terms of capacity—it must also disguise the impetus of feelings. The Hero is a master of ingenuity, who conceals not only his talents but also those things that stir his emotions.

(2) So accredited is this subtle art, that Tiberius and Louis built their entire political machine and policy on it.[3] To hide one's excesses is great wealth and to conceal one's intentions is divine sovereignty.

Ailments of the will and lack of self control are the commencement of a fainting reputation and, once declared, will bring a very public and tragic ending.

(3) The Hero moves to violate and tame his defects first and to conceal them second. The former requires courage, and the latter requires cunning.

Those who surrender to their defects descend from men to brutes, but those who rebuff them retain, at least in appearance, their reputation.

---

[3] A reference to Tiberius Caesar Augustus and King Louis XI of France.

(4) Eminence argues to penetrate all foreign will, while superiority knows how to conceal its own.

(5) It is the same to discover the affections of a man as it is to open a door to the fortress of his wealth, for there the attentive Heroes scheme politically, and most of the time they assail with triumph. To know the affections of a man is to know the entrances and exits of his will, lording over him at all times.

The inhumanity of antiquity conceived gods out of people with less than half the exploits of the great Alexander, and they offered the unvanquished Macedonian laurels but denied him the title of host of deities. He, who conquered so much of the world, was given so little of heaven; why so much scarcity when he was so abundant?

(6) Alexander tarnished the illustriousness of his prowess with the vulgarity of his fury; and he denied himself, so often triumphant, by surrendering to the avariciousness and greed of passion. It did him little good to conquer the world, because he lost the patrimony of a prince, which is reputation.

Excellence steers its course between the desire of Charybdis and the anger of Scylla, to protect its reputation.[4]

Let the Hero then, firstly, take heed and violate his passions or, at least, conceal them with such cunning that no counterattack may succeed in deciphering his will.

This ruse teaches one to understand but not to be understood; and then, it goes on to hide every defect, denying the watchtowers of carelessness and dazzling the lynxes of obscurity.

---

4 **Charybdis and Scylla, in Greek mythology, were two immortal monsters who beset the narrow waters traversed by the hero Odysseus.**

(7) That Catholic Amazon, Queen Isabella, for whom Spain did not have to envy the other queens of the world, was an oracle of these subtleties. She would shut herself up to give birth in the darkest chambers of the palace, and, jealous of connatural decorum, her majesty would seal her sighs in her royal bosom, without a woe being heard, and in a veil of darkness to cover the momentary excesses of her countenance. And if she was so cunning in worthless matters that would not fault her modesty, how much more so in matters upon which staked her reputation?

Cardinal Madrucius did not classify as foolish the one who aborts a folly, but rather the one who, having committed it, does not know how to suffocate it.

(8) Ever accessible is primness and excellence to a silent man; qualified as a natural inclination and improved through diligence; a pledge of divinity, if not by nature, by resemblance.

-III-

Ingenuity: The Hero's Greatest Strength

Just as great parts are a prerequisite for a great whole, great ingenuity is a prerequisite for the engineering of a Valiant Hero.

The astute and discerning give the most importance to having a prodigious perspicacity, because it is the origin of all greatness; and, just as they do not know a great man who is without excesses in understanding, so too do they not know a man excessively knowledgeable without greatness.

(1) Man is the best of the visible world because of his capacity for understanding: his triumphs and accomplishments qualify this greatness with proof.

(2) This capital is the adaptation of two other qualities: great depths of discernment and an elevation of ingenuity, which, together, form a prodigy of keen understanding.

(3) If philosophy prodigiously requires the two great powers of memory and understanding, then governing, even more rightfully, demands judgment and ingenuity, seated between synderesis[5] and acuity.

---
5 Synderesis: an inborn knowledge of the primary principles of moral action.

Only this very distinct intelligence, alone, can pass scrupulous truth and condemn so many variations of behavior as confusion of the mind with the will.

Discernment is the throne of prudence, and Ingenuity is the sphere of sagacity. Which is to be preferred, then, and in what proportion, eminence or moderation? That, is a matter for the court of personal taste. Personally, I am with the woman who prayed, "My son, may Heaven grant you the understanding of the divine."

(4) The bravery, the promptness, and the subtlety of ingenuity are, like the sun or lightning, glimpses of divinity. Every Hero has had a prodigious excess of it.

Caesar's sayings are the splendors of his deeds. He was soon equal to the great Alexander both in thinking and in doing.

And, in continuing to appreciate the true Heroes, Augustine's acuity was equal to his acuteness; and in Charles V, the Holy Roman Emperor, discernment and perseverance were in competition.

(5) Great are the promptings of ingenuity, and random are those of the will. Discernment is the wings of greatness, with which many have soared in lucidity from the center of the dust to the sun.

There was once a great Turkish king, shackled by decorum and a prisoner of his own majesty, who deigned to appear on a balcony overlooking the commoners in a garden rather than the public square. As he began to read a paper, God, either as a joke or as a reminder of his sovereignty over all, sent the wind to snatch it away and carry it into the trees. At once, the king's pages, trying to outdo themselves and the wind, flew down the ladder on the wings of flattery. One of them, named Ganime, in his cleverness, knew how to find a shortcut through the air, and he threw himself over the balcony. He flew, caught the paper, and took it back to the king as the others were still coming down. Because of this, he rose in rank and even soared, because the king, effectively flattered, lifted him up to his own valor. Ingenuity is the offspring of the divine, but it is not personified and seeks to showcase itself through the discerning acts of a Hero.

(6) It is in every fiber of every gift, the great promulgator of fame and reputation; and the deeper its foundation, the more it will proclaim its possessor.

Ingenuity is the crowned champion of wit, even in the ordinary sayings of a king. The great treasures of monarchs may perish, but their witty proverbs are preserved in the golden boxes of fame.

(7) It was worth more to many of the sons of fame than perhaps all the iron in their armed shields, the reward for their shrewdness being a permanent place in history's halls of greatness.

Ingenuity! An exclamation and a proclamation, of the greatest credit, in the kings of wisdom and in the wisest of kings, serving them with judicious promptness in the extremities of litigation; a gift from Heaven, which they used to balance the scales of justice.

And even in barbarous tribunals, ingenuity shines brighter than the sun. The astuteness of the great Turk rivals that of Solomon. A Jew wanted to cut an ounce of flesh from a Christian as payment for interest on a loan, a penalty of usury. He insisted on it, as vehement towards the king as he was contemptuous towards Christ. The sagacious judge then commanded that a weight and a knife be brought into the court, and threatened the Jew with a slow and painful death if he cut more or less than an exact ounce. He dealt with the injustice masterfully and gave the world a glimpse of the miracle of ingenuity.

(8) Ingenuity is an oracle in the midst of the greatest doubts, a sphinx in the enigmas of life, a golden thread in aberrations; but like a lion, it usually waits until the most difficult of situations to show its best.

(9) But there are those who use their ingenuity as foolishly as some use their fortunes. Too blind to honor the Holy One, they routinely embrace the vileness of vice. If the cruel are kneaded with blood, they are kneaded with venom. In them, the laws of nature are confounded, and they are sentenced to an abyss of scorn and contempt for the misuse of this precious gift.

(10) Favor of nature, but also an enhancement of art. Nature engenders acuity, but diligence nourishes it; sometimes, from the salt of personal experience; sometimes, from the salt of others; and other times, from the salt of anticipation, through study and observation.

The sagacious proverbs and deeds of antiquity's finest kings are, in a fertile capacity, seeds of ingenuity from which, once fertilized by acuity, multiply the harvest and promptly produce an abundance of greatness in the Hero.

As for Discernment, he needs no advocacy, for he speaks for himself.

-IV-

The Heart of a King

(1) Philosophers have great heads; orators, great tongues; athletes, great chests; soldiers, armaments; couriers, feet; porters, shoulders. Kings, great hearts. This, according to Plato's politics and divinities, writings that some use to argue which is more favorable: having a great heart or great intelligence.

(2) What does it matter if great understanding goes forward, if a fearful heart holds back? The mind often conceives sweetly what the heart finds difficult to bring to pass.

The subtleties of thought are, for the most part, sterile and are further weakened by timidity in execution.

Great results come from a great cause, by the feats of great deeds, and from a prodigy of the greatest heart. The children of a great heart are giants; they always presume to engage in undertakings equal to their courage and affect first affairs.

Great was the heart of Alexander; just a tiny part of it was enough to conquer the world, and another six if they existed.

(3) But maximum was the heart of the Great Emperor, who knew no middle ground and whose example should fill our hearts with determination—either the heart of Caesar, or nothing.

The heart is the stomach of fortune, which digests her extremes with equal courage. A great stomach does not become full from either large amounts of fortune or misfortune; it is not easily choked with affectation, nor is it troubled with ingratitude. The hunger of a giant is the overindulgence of a dwarf.

(4) The miracle of courage, I say, was the Dauphin of France King Charles VII, called the Victorious. His valor was pressed to its extremities when his father disinherited him, announcing that he would not ascend to the throne, even as the Kingdom of England and the Duke of Burgundy were simultaneously occupying most of France, including Paris. Undismayed, he announced that he would appeal both his father's decision and England's current occupation. "But to whom?" they asked. "To the greatness of my heart and the point of my sword," he responded. And so he did.

The most eternal diamond does not shine as brightly in the midst of burning coal as a determined heart does in the midst of the violence of risk.

(5) The modern Achilles, Carlos Manuel de Saboya, the Duke of Savoy, broke through four hundred enemy armored soldiers with only four of his own and satiated universal admiration, saying, "there is no ally in the greatest predicament like that of a great heart."

The surplus of it makes up for the lack of everything else, being always the first to reach a difficulty and winning.

(6) The King of Arabia was once presented with a scimitar made of Damascus steel. His court praised it as being like a lightning bolt of steel but lamented it was too short for warfare. The king then sent for the prince to give his vote, and he could, for he was the famous Jacob Almanzor. The prince examined it and found everything pertaining to it to be in

excess. "But all of these men condemn it as being too short," said the king, to which the prince responded, "For a valiant knight, there is never a short weapon; for if he takes a step forward, he lengthens it considerably, and what he lacks in steel, his heart makes up for in courage."

(7) Heaven crowns this gift with laurels when an offense is met with magnanimity. Emperor Hadrian taught us a rare and excellent way to triumph over our enemies when he stood over his conquered nemesis and said, "You seemed to have escaped."

There is no admiration equal to that which King Louis XII of France deserves when he said—"You have nothing to fear. I, the King of France, do not avenge the injuries done to me as the Duke of Orleans." These are the miracles that the heart of a Valiant Hero produces.

-V-

A Man of Relevant Taste

(1) Those of great capacity are never satisfied. Taste must be disciplined and refined no less than ingenuity, as they are both extremely pertinent, greatly aiding the Hero during the crucibles of life; they are brothers of one womb, children of ability, sharing equally in the inheritance of excellence.

Sublime ingenuity can never produce barbaric taste.

(2) Perfect are the rays of the sun, and mediocre are the illuminations of a lantern. Yet, while the eagle soars to court the sun, the little worm squirms trying to escape the light of a lamp. To measure the depths of someone's greatness, take notice of their taste.

It is important to have, even more so when it is relevant. And since it easily transmits from one person to another, it is considered great luck to meet someone who has it as a superlative.

Many believe that happiness means finally enjoying what they have desired (I consider this borrowed bliss) and condemn others to unhappiness; but those others retaliate, reminding the former that fortune will soon take back what they have so longed to possess. And so what we see is each half of the world laughing at one another, both fully committed to foolishness.

(3) It is a quality of the divine to have discerning taste, a palate difficult to satisfy: the most desired objects fear it, and the surest perfections tremble before it.

(4) Taste determines esteem, the daughter of preciousness, and only the discreet know how to bargain with it. Be scarce with the currency of applause, and it will seem generous when received. But waste your esteem, and you will receive the punishment of contempt.

Ignorance and admiration are easily, and very frequently, confused; the latter is born not out of perfection but from the imperfect judgment of humans. Perfections of the first magnitude are unique; therefore, let your appreciation be rare and your applause even rarer.

(5) One who truly had the taste of a king was the prudent King Philip II of Spain, who was accustomed to seeing miraculous objects and only paid attention to things that were truly unique marvels.

A Portuguese merchant presented him with a star of the earth, a very precious and exquisite Oriental diamond; a cipher of wealth and a wonder of splendor. As everyone was expecting to hear admiration or, at the very least, interest from Philip, they heard disdain instead; not because the great monarch was affected by the unseemly or the serious, but because a taste so accustomed to miracles of nature and art does not awe so vulgarly. What a moment of extremity for this well-intentioned merchant.

"Sire," he said, "seventy thousand ducats I spent on this worthy grandson of the sun; please do not be offended." King Philip pressed the point and said to him, "What were you thinking of when you paid so much?" "Sire," said the Portuguese, "I was thinking that there was a King Philip II in the world." The monarch was more impressed with the sharpness of his wit than with the preciousness of the stone, and he ordered to pay him the diamond and to reward him for his clever retort: showing the superiority of his taste, in the price and in the prize.

Some feel that he who does not exceedingly praise condemns. I say, however, that the surplus of praise implies a lack of discernment and that he who praises too much is either making fun of himself or others.

King Agesilaus would not deign a compliment even to the one who could fit the shoe of Enceladus to a pygmy;[6] in matters of praise, it is an art to measure precisely.

(6) The world was full of the exploits of the one who was the dawn of the greatest sun, known as the Grand Duke of Alba in Spain and the Iron Duke in Portugal, the indomitable Don Fernando Alvarez de Toledo; and while he conquered the world, he never meditated on his conquests. He once said that "in forty years of victory, having all of Europe as my battlefield and all the armies of my time on exhibit, it all seems like nothing; because I have never seen an army like that of the Turks in battle, one against whom victory would be a triumph of skill and not of strength, where humiliating that excessive power would exalt my experience and courage as a leader." So much is necessary to silence the taste of the Valiant Hero.

---

[6] Here, Gracián says that King Agesilaus, Sparta's most famous ruler, would not even be impressed by the one who could fit the shoe of a mythical giant to the foot of a human dwarf.

(7) To polish this primness is not to go from a cultured man to a *momo*,[7] which is an insufferable intemperance, but to be an integral censor of what is truly worthy. Some enslave their judgment to preconceptions, favoritism, and affectations, thereby preventing impeccable discernment from differentiating between the light and the darkness.

(8) Learn to esteem each thing for itself; do not allow your judgment to be bribed.

(9) Only great knowledge, aided by great experience, can correctly assess the price of perfection. And where the prudent man cannot effortlessly cast his vote of discernment, let him pause: lest he reveal the poverty of his judgment by praising the strangeness of another.

---

7 "Momo" is Spanish slang for idiot or clown.

-VI-

A Man of Eminence

(1) To embrace and encompass all perfection is only granted to the First Being, who, not receiving it from another, suffers no limitations.[8]

(2) Some gifts are given to us by Heaven, others are gained through effort; one or two are not sufficient to enhance a man; so when Heaven deprives you of natural ones, let your diligence supply acquired ones. The former are daughters of favor; the latter, of praiseworthy effort and determination and are not usually the least noble.

(3) Only a little is needed to be an average individual; much, to be a universal man; and so rare are the latter that they are often denied reality and instead relegated to conceptualization.

There is not one eminence that is worth many. Great excellence of an intense singularity encodes entire categories, equally.

Not all art deserves esteem, and not all work achieves credit. To know everything repels criticism; but to talk about everything is to sin against reputation.

---
[8] A reference to Jesus Christ.

To be eminent in a humble profession is to be great in little, to be something in nothing. To remain average courts indolence; to become eminent challenges fear.

(4) The two Philips, that of Spain and Macedonia, were very different.[9] The first was second only in name and first in all else. It was the former who corrected the prince for singing in the chambers and the latter who asked Alexander to run in the Olympic Games. One showed the discernment of prudence, and the other showed the carelessness of greatness. Why should Alexander have competed with men who were not kings?

Commonly, what has more of the delightful has less of the heroic.

(5) The Hero should aspire to be a maximum man and should not limit himself to one perfection or another but, with ambitions of infinity, aspire to a plausible universality, and the more important the art, the more intense his knowledge of it.

(6) Slight cognition of a subject is not sufficient. Attentive males will quickly condemn you for being more talkative than learned. This is a matter of fundamental integrity.

(7) To attain eminence in everything is impossible to say the least—not because of weakness of ambition, but of diligence and even of life. Repetition is the means for the consummation of what one professes, but all things require time, and in that process, we lose our desire for what we once aspired.

Many mediocrities are not enough to add greatness, but only one eminence is enough to assure superiority.

---
9 A reference to King Philip II of Spain, known as the Prudent, and Philip II of Macedon, father of Alexander the Great.

(8) There can be no Hero without eminence in something, because it is the character of greatness; and the more qualified the job, the more thunderous the applause. Eminence is a precious jewel, related by blood to sovereignty, and when it arrives, it crowns its master with veneration.

And if one can win praise by being eminent in kicking a ball into the wind, what will he attain if he is eminent with a sword, a pen, a rod, a scepter, or a crown?

(9) That Castilian Mars,[10] by whom it was said, "Castilla for captains and Aragón for kings," Don Diego Perez de Vargas, with more exploits than days, retired after finishing the Moors in the Battle of Jerez. He retired, but not his fame, which every day spread more and more throughout the universe. One day, the Magnanimous King Alfonso V, an old admirer of eminence and arms, went to look for him in disguise with only four knights.

Marvelous eminence, it is a magnet of wills and a spell of affection.

When the king arrived at Jerez, he went to Vargas' home but did not find him there, because the Hero, who was so used to battle, was on his warhorse, riding in the open air, with a sword in his hand, pruning his vines. When the king saw him, he ordered his men to hide and rode by himself towards the warrior. He dismounted his horse and, with majestic gallantry, began to pick up the vine shoots that Vargas was knocking down. The Valiant Knight turned his head, alerted by the noise made by the king or, what is more certain, by some faithful impulse of his heart; and when he saw his majesty, he threw himself at his feet and said,

"Sire, what are you doing here?" "Go on, Vargas," said King Alfonso. "I hope I am worthy to gather your vines."

---
10 **Mars is the Roman god of war.**

Oh! The triumph of eminence!

Let the rare man thirst for it, certain that what it will cost him in fatigue will be repaid with fame.

Antiquity was right to consecrate with gentility an ox to Hercules. The praiseworthy work of sowing exploits promises a harvest of fame, of applause, and of immortality.

-VII-

The Excellence of Being First

(1) Some of them would have been a phoenix of occupation if others had not gone before them. It is a great advantage to be first; and, if with eminence, double the advantage. The winner is the one who deals the first hand and gains the upper ground.

Those who follow are considered to be imitators of the past; and, however much they sweat, they cannot purge that presumption of imitation. The first ones are raised on the estate of fame, and the second ones are left with table scraps.

Antiquity ceased to esteem the inventors of the arts and began to venerate them. They turned esteem into worship; an ordinary error, but one that shows how important it is to be first.

(2) However, the trick is not to be the first in time but to be the first in eminence.

(3) Plurality discredits itself, even in precious carats; and, conversely, rarity makes moderate perfection more expensive.

It is, therefore, an uncommon skill to invent a new path to excellence, to discover a modern course for celebrity. There are many paths that lead to singularity, and not all of them are well trodden. The newest, though arduous, are usually the shortcuts to greatness.

(4) Solomon wisely chose wisdom, yielding bellicosity to his father the warrior. He changed course and arrived with less difficulty at the mountaintop of Heroes.

Tiberius did with politics what Augustus did with magnanimity.

And our great Philip II, who ruled from his throne of prudence the whole world, to the astonishment of all centuries. If Emperor Caesar, the unconquered patriarch of kings, was a prodigy of determination, Philip was a prodigy of prudence.

Many sons of the Church ascended, in this same manner, to the zenith of celebrity. Some became eminent through their piety, others by being supremely learned; some by the magnificence of the structures they erected, and others by knowing how to enhance the positions they held.

With this novelty of matters, those who were noticed have always made a place for themselves on the register of greatness.

Without leaving their art, the wise know how to go out of the ordinary and find a new way to engage even the gray-haired professions, stepping into the rays of eminence. Horace gave heroic poetry to Virgil, and Martial gave the lyric to Horace. Terence embraced the comedic and Persius the satirical, each one aspiring to the fame of being first in their genre: bold ideas never surrendered to easy imitation.

(5) That gallant painter Diego de Velazquez saw that Titian, Raphael, and others were impossible to overtake in greatness; their fame had become more alive after their deaths. He made use of his invincible inventiveness and started

to paint in a bold style. When some objected that he did not paint smooth and polished, in emulation of Titian, he responded, "I would rather be the first in coarseness than the second in delicacy."

(6) Let this example be extended to all occupations, and let every Hero understand this perfect strategy: that in eminent novelty he will find an uncommon path to greatness.

-VIII-
May the Hero Prefer Reasonable Endeavors

(1) Two homelands produced two Heroes: Thebes, Hercules; and Rome, Cato. Hercules was applauded by the world, and Cato was an annoyance to Rome. Hercules was admired by all peoples; Cato was scorned by the Romans.

(2) The advantage that Cato had over Hercules is uncontroversial, for he exceeded him in prudence; but Hercules bested Cato in fame.

Cato's undertaking was more arduous and exquisite, since he insisted on taming monsters of habit and Hercules those of nature; but the Theban's was still more famous.[11]

---

11 Father Gracian contrasts the life trajectories of two "heroes," one mythological and the other historical. Hercules was known and admired throughout the world; Cato was hardly known beyond Rome. The difference, according to him, is marked by the fact that the twelve labors of Hercules (the Lion of Nemea, the Hydra of Lerna, etc.) are much more "reasonable" successes, to the taste and understanding of the majority. In contrast, Cato's efforts to uphold Roman values, combat Greek influence, and expose corruption within the Senate were met with resistance and disapproval (he insisted on taming monsters of habit). Despite his exceptional leadership as tribune and censor, Cato's dedication to noble causes left him overshadowed by the more sensational exploits of Hercules.

(3) The difference consists in the fact that Hercules undertook admirable exploits and Cato odious ones. The praiseworthy undertakings of Hercules brought his glory to the ends of the world and would have gone even further if the world had been lengthened. But the unpleasantness of Cato's endeavors enclosed him within the walls of Rome.

(4) With all this, some, including judicious ones, still prefer a difficult matter to the most reasonable; the admiration of a few does more for them than the applause of many, if vulgar.

To them, deeds that win widespread applause are "miracles of the ignorant."

(5) The arduous, those primordial circumstances of a superiorly difficult matter, are perceived by few, and these few are as eminent as they are rare. And the rarity of these Heroes is what gives those difficult circumstances their value, more so than the actual circumstances themselves. Furthermore, an easy circumstance makes everyone capable of it, and any applause is worth nothing.

The undertakings of the discerning few prevails over the vulgarity of the majority.

(6) It is a great skill to find praiseworthy undertakings, but a matter of discretion and prudence to bribe for common attention, which is, at times, necessary. To win the approval of the majority, regardless of the undertaking, immortalizes a Valiant Hero.

(7) Many times, in public matters of a reasonable nature, eminence is a matter of public opinion; and the opinion of the majority is esteemed.

(8) In these instances, the most esteemed matters should be esteemed more. They are almost palpable. The fervor of

public opinion makes them tangible and, if the Hero conquers them with evidence, mesmerizing.

Matters well discerned are always the most beautiful and carry with them the metaphysical, conquering interpretation and opinion.

(9) I call reasonable endeavors those that are executed in the sight of all and to the liking of all, with mindfulness always on one's reputation. I would exclude all that lack honor or are in excess of ostentation; in life, reputation is a matter of life or death.

(10) To be, then, eminent in a noble matter, exposed to the universal theater, is to achieve perfect discernment in choosing.

(11) What princes occupy the catalogs of fame, if not warriors? They are owed the title of Great. They fill the world with applause, the centuries with fame, and the books with their prowess; in this world, the warlike garner more praise than the peaceful.

(12) Among the judges, the strictest and the most just live in immortality, because justice without cruelty was always more acceptable to the vulgar than mercy remiss.

In matters of wit, reason has always triumphed. The sweetness of a sagacious speech freshens the soul and flatters the ear, whereas the dryness of a metaphysical concept torments and angers.

-IX-

The Most Precious Diamond

(1) I do not know whether to call it intelligence or luck when the Hero comes across his greatest talent, that most precious diamond, the king attribute of his wealth.

In some Heroes, the heart reigns, and in others, the head; discover your greatest talent, because it would be a point of folly for one to study with courage and another to fight with wit.

Let the peacock be content with his wheel of plumage and the eagle with his flight: it would be a great monstrosity for the ostrich to aspire to soar, exposed to an exemplary fall; let him console himself with the bizarreness of his feathers.

(2) There is no man who, in some undertaking, cannot achieve some success. But very few are those who excel and achieve true eminence; these are considered very rare, both unique and excellent, and like the phoenix, their excellence is always anticipated.

No man considers himself unskilled; self-flattery always leads to deceptions of effort. But Chronos[12] disabuses all,

---
12 Chronos is the personification of time in pre-Socratic philosophy and later literature.

and eventually one has to admit that perhaps he did the job well, but he did not reach the peak of perfection.

(3) Better to be eminent in the mediocre than mediocre in the eminent. And it is intolerable to be mediocre in the least important when you can be first in the most sublime.

(4) He who taught the truth, although a poet,[13] once said, "Do not undertake any endeavor that Minerva[14] contradicts." There is nothing more difficult than to disabuse a man of his own capacity.

Oh, if there were mirrors for understanding, as there are for the face. Understanding must be its own looking glass, but it is easily falsified and tarnished. Every judge of himself is quick to find a pretext for escape by taking bribes from his own emotions.

(5) Extraordinary are the variety of inclinations—delightful prodigies of nature—as great as the variety of faces, voices, and temperaments that Heaven created.

There are as many talents as there are occupations. And even the most vile and even infamous are not lacking in passionate proponents. And so, the talents that Almighty Providence cannot voluntarily bring forth from the most political king, it must facilitate through the enticement of his inclinations.

If a monarch had to distribute menial tasks, "You, be a farmer, and you, be a sailor," he would quickly surrender to impossibility and despair; no one would be happy even with the most civil of tasks or occupations; but left up to his own choice, man is blindly attracted to even the lowest, most villainous, and most detestable.

---
13   A reference to the poet Horace.
14   Minerva is the Roman goddess of wisdom.

(6) Powerful are inclinations; and, together with talent, they form an invincible force. But the usual thing is to be dissatisfied.

Therefore, let the prudent man flatter his taste and direct his natural talent without the violence of despotism, aligning it with his inclinations to measure his strength; and once recognized, put it to work in his favor.

(7) The prodigious Marquis of the Valley, Don Hernán Cortés,[15] would never have become a Spanish Alexander and an Indian Caesar if he had not shuffled between employments and undertakings; as a writer, he would have, at most, reached a very vulgar mediocrity; but through the force of arms, he climbed to the summit of eminence, forming a trifecta with Alexander and Caesar, dividing among the three the conquest of the world by their parts.

---

15   Hernán Cortés was the Spanish conquistador who began the Spanish colonization of the Americas.

-X-

May the Hero Test His Fortune Before Committing Himself

Fortune, who is so talked about and so little understood, is none other, speaking in a sane and even Catholic way, than that great mother of contingencies and great daughter of Supreme Providence, who is never absent from her post, sometimes allowing and other times refusing.

She is that sovereign queen: inscrutable and inexorable, smiling on one, burdensome on another, a mother to some, a stepmother to others, and not by emotions but by the arcanity of her inaccessible, mysterious judgments, which are a reflection of Heaven's divine will.

The masters of political discretion have always observed their fortune and that of their men. And those who experience her as a mother should receive her gifts and commit themselves boldly. She loves to be flattered by trust.

(1) Caesar had his finger on the pulse of his fortune when, encouraging the surrendered ferryman, he said to him: "Fear not, for you are insulting Caesar's fortune." There was no surer anchor for his confidence than this. The Emperor carried in his stern the breaths of fortune and did not fear the contrary winds. What do gales matter, if the sky is serene? And who cares that the sea roars, if the stars laugh?

(2) What seemed to many like a reckless endeavor was really nothing more than dexterity and a perfect understanding of the favor of his fortune. Others, however, have lost great opportunities for notability, because they did not understand their fortune. Even the blind gambler consults his luck before he throws the dice.

(3) It is a great gift to be a fortunate man, and, in the estimation of many, the greatest of gifts. Some esteem an ounce of fortune more than a pound of wisdom or a hundred of courage; others still, base their reputation on misfortune and melancholy. Oh, the luck of fools! To find distinction in disgrace!

Like the sagacious father who makes up for the ugliness of his daughter by adorning her with gold, the universe decorates the ugliness of their ingenuity with luck.

(4) Galen had fortune as his physician;[16] Vegetius had her as his captain;[17] and Aristotle, as his monarch.[18] One thing is certain: every Valiant Hero is sponsored by courage and fortune, the twin axes of heroism.

(5) But he who has fortune as a bitter stepmother, let him be gentle in his endeavors and not stubborn, for her disfavor is heavier than lead.

---

16 Aelius Galenus, most often anglicized as Galen, was a Roman and Greek physician, surgeon, and philosopher. Considered one of the foremost medical researchers of antiquity, Galen influenced the development of several scientific disciplines, such as anatomy, physiology, pathology, pharmacology, and neurology, as well as philosophy and logic.

17 Publius Vegetius was a writer in the later part of the Roman Empire. Little is known of him other than his treatise on military warfare, titled "*De re militari,*" Latin for "Concerning Military Matters."

18 Aristotle is considered to be the most important thinker who ever lived.

And at this point, let me pretend to steal the saying of the eloquent poet, with the obligation to modify its advice for the lovers of prudence: "Do not do or say anything while fortune is against you."[19]

(6) I say, with happiness and with evidence of his splendor, the Benjamin[20] of today is the heroic, undefeated, and most serene Lord: the Cardinal-Infante of Spain, Don Fernando,[21] a name that should become the coat of arms for the Valiant Hero.

The whole world was held in suspense by fortune's love for him; satisfied with his courage, the great queen declared him her gallant knight on the very first occasion; she became immortal to him and deadly to his enemies, giving him complete and total victory in the battle of Norlingen, total dominance in countless battles in France and Flanders, and spreading the rest of her favor for him in Jerusalem.

(7) It is part of political skill to discern when fortune is for or against you, so you can know when to engage and when to yield in competition.

Suleiman foresaw that great fortune favored our Catholic Mars, Charles V, and feared her more than all the armies of the king.[22]

---

19 See footnote thirteen.

20 The name Benjamin means "son of the right hand."

21 Don Fernando of Austria was a Spanish and Portuguese Prince, Governor of the Spanish Netherlands, Cardinal of the Holy Catholic Church, Archduke of Austria, Archbishop of Toledo, and general during the Thirty Year War, Eighty Year War, and Franco-Spanish War. He is often considered the last great commander and strategist of the Spanish Empire, and he is one of the few generals in history who is undefeated in battle.

22 A reference to the Battle of Pavia, in which Suleiman the Magnificent was allied with King Francis I against King Charles V.

And while he could not save his reputation, because he had already retreated, he at least saved his crown.

But this was not so with Francis of France, who chose to ignore his own fortune and that of our Caesar and thus was sentenced to prison for offending prudence.[23]

(8) The prosperous or adversarial nature of fortune is usually attached to an individual and always at his side. Understand then, Discreet Man and Valiant Hero, that in the game of triumph, you must discern when to engage and disengage to achieve victory.

23　A reference to the capture and imprisonment of King Francis after losing the Battle of Pavia.

-XI-
May the Hero Know When to Retire, with Fortune at His Side

(1) Everything in motion must fluctuate, rise, and decline. Those who fail to comprehend this will only dwell in instability.

Great providence is to know how to prevent the infallible decline of fortune's restless wheel. The subtlety of a *tahúr*[24] is needed to know how to leave with a profit, because where prosperity is a game, misfortune is always present.

It is better to leave with honor than to wait for fortune's whirlwind, which tends to win with a single stroke all that you gained from many sets.[25]

(2) She has a lack of consistency and an overabundance of feminine energy say those whom she has scathed. And the

---

24 *Tahúr* is Spanish slang for a gambler or, more specifically, a cardsharp: someone who is a master of playing cards and is so skilled that he can cheat without anyone noticing.

25 Here, Father Gracián tells us to be a *tahúr* when engaging life's circumstances. To defeat the ever-present threat of misfortune, we must not only know which cards to keep and which to discard, but also, master the art of knowing when to quit.

Marquis of Mariñano[26] added, for the consolation of the Emperor at Metz, that she has not only the instability of a woman but also the whims of a flirtatious young girl.

(3) But I say that these are not the variations of a woman but the alternations of a most just Providence.

(4) Let the Hero succeed in this: let him retire to the sacred place of an honorable retreat, given that a beautiful retreat is as glorious as a gallant attack.

But there are hydropics of luck who thirst for fortune and who have no courage to overcome their lack of self-control once they get a taste of her water.

Let the great master of fortune and luck, Charles V, the greatest of all the Charles' and even of Heroes, be an impressive example of this preeminence. This most glorious emperor crowned with prudent ends all of his exploits. He triumphed over the entire world with fortune, and then, in the end, he triumphed over fortune herself. He knew how to retire, setting the seal of greatness on his prowess.[27]

(5) Others, however, lost all the wealth of their fame as a penalty of their greed. They had a monstrous end to the great beginnings of their happiness, when, had they used this trick, they could have secured their reputation.

The ring that was thrown into the sea and discovered in the belly of a fish was a token of inseparability between

---

26 A reference to Gian Giacomo Medici, the Italian mercenary who became an Italian and Spanish general. He was in the service of King Charles V during the Battle of Metz, one of the few battles the Emperor lost.

27 A reference to the Emperor abdicating his throne and retiring to the monastery of Yuste.

Polycrates and Fortune. But soon after came the tragic theater of their divorce at Mount Micalense.[28]

So that others could open their eyes, Belisarius was blinded;[29] so that many could see the light, the Moon of Spain was eclipsed.[30] [31]

(6) There is no art that can take the pulse of fortune, because her mood is anomalous; therefore, we must learn to foresee the signs of her declining favor.

Sudden prosperity, where one happiness overlaps the other, has always been suspicious; fortune's benevolence tends to be very short-lived. She likes to quickly curtail what has accumulated from her favor.

Fortune that has grown old nears its expiration date, while extremes of misfortune often mean a stroke of good luck is nearby.

(7) The Moor Abul, brother of the king of Granada, was imprisoned in Salobreña, and to deny his confirmed misfortunes, he began to play chess, a game of fortune.

---

28 A reference to the legend of the Polycrates Ring. According to the Greek historian Herodotus, King Polycrates, believing himself too successful, sought to throw away that which he valued most in order to escape a reversal of fortune. So he threw a jewel-encrusted ring into the sea; however, a few days later, a fisherman caught a large fish that he wished to share with the king. While the fish was being prepared, the ring was discovered inside its belly. Shortly thereafter, Polycrates was defeated in battle and crucified.

29 A reference to the Legend of the Blind Beggar, where Emperor Justinian is said to have ordered Belisarius' eyes be removed and reduced him to the status of a homeless beggar before pardoning him for treason.

30 A reference to Álvaro de Luna (*luna* is Spanish for moon), a Spanish Count who was executed after losing favor in the court of King Juan II of Castilla.

31 Learn from the misfortune of other men, so that you are not as unfortunate.

While playing, a messenger arrived who instructed him that he should prepare to die; death always seems to arrive unsuspectingly. Abul asked for two more hours of life, but the commissioner thought it was too long and granted him only to finish the game he had begun. He was lucky and won his life and even the kingdom; because before it finished, another messenger arrived with news of life and crown: the king was dead, and he was next in line for the throne of Granada.

As many went up from the knife to the crown as came down from the crown to the knife. Savor the good morsels of luck, even when they are accompanied by the bittersweetness of chance and challenges.

(8) Fortune is a pirate, waiting for the ships to load; so let this be your counterstrategy: anticipate when to take port.

-XII-

Winning the Grace of Others

(1) It is a negligible thing to win an argument if goodwill is not won; and a significant victory if admiration and affection are won together.

Many, with plausible ventures, maintain credit but not benevolence.

(2) To obtain universal favor requires, at the very least, a lucky star; and, at the very most, one's own diligence. Others will argue the opposite when, although equal in merit to another, their corresponding applause is disproportionately less.

Also, the same thing that one uses to magnetize the will serves another as a repellent. Here, I will always give the upper hand to artifice.

(3) The eminence of talents and gifts is not enough to win the gratitude of people, although it is supposed to be. It is easiest to win affection when opinion is bribed; because esteem is the cause of affection.

(4) The Duke of Guise,[32] famously acclaimed and rich in admiration, executed masterfully for this common grace, though he received no favor from his king, the third of the French Henry's—fatal name for a prince in any monarchy; astounding that in such high subjects even the names decipher oracles.

One day this king asked his followers: What does Guise do to bewitch the people? —Answered one, whose sincerity would make him unique in these times: —Sire, to do good, by all means: those who his benevolent influences do not reach directly they reach by reflection; and when not by works, by words. There is no wedding he does not celebrate, no baptism he does not sponsor, no burial he does not honor; he is courteous, humane, generous, an honorer of all, a murmurer of none; and, in short, he is the king by affection, like your majesty is by law.

Happy grace if he would have deflected the admiration to his king; after all, there was no need for competition. However, some say the opposite, and the applause granted to a servant will always make the master jealous.

Truly, I say, that of God, of the king, and of the people are the three most important graces, more so than any grace the ancients could have imagined. They shake hands, each one with the others, and if any of them must go missing, let it be in reverse order.

(5) The most powerful spell to be loved is to love. It is rapturous, relentless in pursuit.

---

32 Henry de Lorraine, the 3rd Duke of Guise, was a popular duke and the acknowledged head of the Catholic party and of the Holy League during the French Wars of Religion. He was assassinated by King Henry III of France, who was jealous of his popularity.

The first advisors in Fortune's entourage, after Opinion, are Courtesy and Generosity; with these two, Emperor Titus came to be known as "the delight of the human race."

A favorable word from a superior is equal to the deed of an equal; and an act of courtesy from a prince exceeds any gift from a citizen.

(6) Putting aside his majesty momentarily, the magnanimous one, King Don Alfonso, dismounted his horse to help a peasant, who then helped him conquer the garrisoned walls of Gaeta, which he had not been able to penetrate in many days of bombardment. He entered first the heart of man and then, with triumph, the city.

Even intemperate critics find, if nothing else, the merit of benevolence in great captains and giant Heroes.

I would say that among the plurality of gifts, each one deserving of plausible fame, this one is most pertinent.

(7) There is also the favor of historians, which is to be desired as much as immortality, because their pens are like the wings of fame. They portray not the successes of nature but those of the soul. That phoenix of kings, Matthias Corvinus, glory of Hungary, used to say that the greatness of a hero consisted of two things: doing good deeds and being gracious to writers, because their golden characters bind one to eternity.

-XIII-

The Natural Hero

(1) Naturalness is the soul of every gift, life of every perfection, gallantry of every action, finesse of every word, and bewitchment of every good taste; it is complementary to mysterious explanations and intelligence.

It is the chief enhancement of all enhancements, and it is a formal beauty. Other gifts adorn nature, but naturalness enhances those gifts themselves. So it is the most perfect part of perfection—a transcendent beauty universally admired by all.

(2) It consists in a certain airiness, in an unspeakable gallantry, both in speaking and in doing, and especially in oration.

(3) It is an innate talent, recognizing learned behavior the least. So far, it has never been subject to precepts and is always superior to any art.

(4) Because it robs one of taste, it's been called overpowering; being imperceptible, many call it mysterious; because it encourages, vigorous; it is gallant, so it is seen as bold; being unobstructive, simple: all these names have sought it, in their desire and difficulty to define it.

It is a grievance to confuse naturalness with ease; for it leaves ease far behind and advances towards style and elegance. It supposes disencumbrance and adds perfection.

Actions have their Lucina;[33] and it is owed to naturalness when they come out well and pave the way for their showcasing.

Without it, the best execution is dead; the greatest perfection, tasteless. Nor is it so much of an accident as it is essential; and it not only serves as an ornament but also supports the most important aspects of action.

For if it is the soul of beauty, it is also the spirit of discernment; and if it is the breath of gallantry, it is also the life of courage.

In a warrior, it is the soul of his valor, and in a king, it is the spirit of his prudence.

On the day of a battle, a natural fearlessness is no less recognized than learned dexterity and courage. Natural self-restraint constitutes first a General, lord of himself, and afterwards, a lord of all.

(5) It is not enough to ponder, nor is it enough to appreciate, the unflappable naturalness of that great conqueror of kings, the greatest emulator of Hercules, Don Fernando de Ávalos.[34] The applause in the theater of Pavia[35] was loud.

It is as fearless on horseback as it is majestic on a throne; and even in the pulpit, it will enhance ingenuity.

---

33 Lucina is the Roman goddess of childbirth.

34 Fernando de Ávalos, 5th Marquess of Pescara, was an Italian captain and mercenary of Aragonese (Spanish) origin. He was an important figure in the Italian Wars and the chief commander of the Habsburg armies of King Charles V in Italy during the Habsburg-Valois Wars, defeating the French at the Battle of Pavia.

35 The Battle of Pavia was the decisive engagement of the Italian Wars between the Kingdom of France and the Habsburg Empire of Charles V, Holy Roman Emperor and ruler of Spain, Austria, the Low Countries, and the Two Sicilies. In the four-hour battle, the French army was thoroughly split and defeated. Many of the chief nobles of France were killed, and others, including King Francis himself, were captured.

(6) Heroic was the disentanglement of that French Theseus,[36] Henry the Fourth, who, with the golden threads of naturalness navigated the maze and disentangled himself from that twisted labyrinth.[37]

And who could cast doubt on its political usefulness? When drawing on this mysterious naturalness, the spiritual monarch of the globe was heard to say, "Is there another world I can conquer?"[38]

---

[36] Theseus was a divine hero and the founder of Athens in Greek mythology.

[37] A reference to the wars of religion between the Catholics and Protestants in France, which King Henry IV, baptized Catholic and raised Protestant, was caught in the middle of.

[38] A reference to Alexander the Great.

-XIV-
Born to Command

(1) This delicacy is so subtle that it would run the risk of being metaphysical if curiosity and caution did not strengthen it.

There shines in some men an innate dominion, a secret imperial force that is obeyed without the exteriority of rules and without the art of persuasion.

(2) When the emperor was taken captive by pirate islanders, he was more a lord over them than a prisoner. As the conquered, he commanded, and as the conquerors, they obeyed. He was captive by ceremony and lord by the reality of his supreme power and authority.[39]

---

39 Julius Caesar was once captured by pirates on his way to procure ships from King Nicomedes for his fleet. Unfortunately for his captors, Caesar proved to be a terrible prisoner. At night, he demanded the pirates keep their voices down so he could sleep. During the day, he forced them to listen to the poems and speeches he composed to stave off boredom and berated them as illiterates if they weren't sufficiently impressed. He took charge of their training exercises, always addressed the pirates as subordinates, and even took issue with his own ransom. Feeling the requested twenty talents of silver was too low for someone of his caliber, he urged them to ask for at least fifty. After the ransom was paid and he was set free, Caesar used the ships he received to pursue the pirates, taking back the fifty talents and crucifying every one of them.

This kind of man executes more with a single gesture than others with all of their diligence. Their countenance has a secret vigor, which wins more by submission than by brilliance.

The proudest mind is subjected to them without noticing how, and the most exempt judgment surrenders to them.

(3) They walk among humanity as lions, because they share the lion's most important trait, which is dominion.

In nature, the beasts of prey recognize the lion; and, without having to test his valor, they are forewarned of his ferocity.

(4) Thus, to these Heroes, these kings of nature, respect is advanced by others without a request for collateral.

This precious jewel is the enhancement of a crown; and if the eminence of understanding and the greatness of the heart also correspond with it, the Hero will lack nothing to become a political conqueror.

(5) This jewel was securely enthroned in Don Fernando Álvarez de Toledo,[40] a lord more by nature than by designation. He was great and was born to be greater but ran out of time; even in speech, he could not violate this natural empire.

---

40   Don Fernando Álvarez de Toledo, known as the Grand Duke of Alba in Spain and the Iron Duke in Portugal, was the most important minister of King Philip II. Invincible in battle against the French and Ottomans during his long military career, he was summoned to fight once again at the age of 73 when Portugal was thrown into a succession crisis after the death of King Sebastian. Although ill and advanced in age, the Duke quickly defeated the Portuguese forces at the Battle of Alcântara, and King Philip of Spain was crowned King of Portugal. The king rewarded Don Fernando with the titles of 1st Viceroy and Constable of Portugal in July of 1580, making him second in command after only the king himself. He held both titles until his death only two years later.

(6) It is far from a deceptive importance, from an affected tone—which is the quintessence of abhorrence—and while not so much the case if inherent, it is very close to the edge of anger.

But it maintains its greatest opposition to self-doubt and against the suspicion of one's own self-worth; more so, it counters the distrust in oneself, which is to surrender to the contempt of others.

It was Cato's admonition and the very birth of his own severity: that a man ought to respect himself, and even to fear himself.

He who loses his own fear gives license to others—and with his own permission—to do the same.

-XV-

A Hero of Sublime Sympathy

(1) It is the duty of a Valiant Hero to have sympathy with the Heroes of antiquity. To bask in the sun is enough to make a plant gigantic and its flower the crown of the garden.

(2) Sympathy is one of the sealed wonders of nature, whose effects are the composition of astonishment and the business of admiration.

It consists of a kinship of hearts, while antipathy is the divorce of wills.

In some, they originate from a correspondence in temperament; while in others, from a brotherhood in the stars, orchestrated by Heaven.

Sympathy aspires to work miracles; and antipathy, monstrosities. The wonders of sympathy are not easily understood, and common ignorance reduces them to spells, and vulgarity to hexes.

The most cultured perfection can suffer the scorn of antipathy, while the most uncultured ugliness can achieve refinement through sympathy.

(3) Even between father and children, they claim jurisdiction and execute every day their power, trampling laws and

preventing the privileges of nature and politics. The antipathy of a father will take away a kingdom, while his sympathy will bestow one.

Everything is achieved by the merits of sympathy; it persuades without a need for eloquence, collects as many faculties as desired, and presents memorials of natural harmony.

(4) Enhanced sympathy is the main character trait and north star of heroism, but there are some of secular taste who maintain antipathy with the diamond and sympathy with the iron. Monstrosities of nature that crave dross and find disgust in brilliance.

(5) Louis the Eleventh was, in matters of diplomacy, a royal machine, but, more by his nature than by art, he missed greatness; lacking sympathy, he lost himself in the dregs of political rank.[41]

(6) Great is active sympathy, if it is noble; and greater is passive sympathy, if it is heroic.[42] It beats in preciousness the great stone of the ring of Gyges;[43] and in efficacy, the chains of the Theban.[44]

---

41 A reference to King Louis XI being a cold, secretive, and reclusive man, "lost in the dregs of political rank"; very few mourned him when he passed. However, diplomatically, Gracián has always held Louis XI in high esteem. In his book *El Político: The Perfect King (1640)*, Father Gracián praises his political and diplomatic acumen numerous times.

42 Father Gracián's meaning regarding active and passive sympathy has remained unclear through the ages. In my estimation, he is referring to, at times, emulating the Greatest Heroes in action (active sympathy) and other times feeling what the Greatest Heroes felt (passive sympathy).

43 The Ring of Gynes is a hypothetical magic ring mentioned by the philosopher Plato in his dialogue *The Republic*. It grants its owner the power to become invisible at will.

44 "The chains of the Theban" is a reference to Hercules, the Greek hero who was born in Thebes, and his golden chains.

(7) The propensity to admire great men is easy, but correlation with them is a rarity. Perhaps the heart wails without the mind hearing an echo of correspondence. Sympathy is the very first lesson, the ABCs, in the school of desire.

Let there be, then, skill in discretion, in knowing and using passive sympathy. Let the attentive male beware of this natural spell, and let art (skill) advance what nature began. It is as indiscreet as it is ill-successful to desire to attempt anything without this natural favor, and even more so, to try and conquer faculties without the ammunition of sympathy.

Sympathy is the queen of all gifts, surpassing even the terms of genius; it is a statue of immortality resting on the everlasting foundation of favorable fortune.

This noble promise is sometimes muffled, because the breaths of favor do not reach it. A magnet cannot attract iron outside its vicinity, nor does sympathy work outside the realm of its activity. It relies on approach and proximity; not meddling and distance.

Attention! Aspiring Heroes: in this chapter, there dawns a brilliant sun!

-XVI-
Greatness Renewed

(1) The first efforts are a test of valor, which go out to visit fame and wealth.

Miracles of progress are not enough to enhance ordinary beginnings; and at best, every subsequent effort is a correction of what came before.

(2) An extraordinary endeavor elevates applause and pawns future valor as collateral, daring the Hero to outdo himself.

Suspicion is a reprobate, and if she enters in the beginning, in matters of reputation, contempt will never leave.

(3) Let a Hero dawn with the splendors of the sun. He must always affect great enterprises, but in the beginning, he must be maximum. Ordinary endeavors cannot lead to extravagant credit, nor can pygmy undertakings lead to the accreditation of a giant.

Maximum beginnings are the assurances of reputation; and those of a Hero must be a hundred stadiums higher than the ends of a commoner.

(4) That sun of captains and general of heroes, the valiant Count of Fuentes,[45] was born to the applause of the rays of the sun; a giant of the utmost lucidity.

His first undertaking may have been the *ne plus ultra* of a Mars: He never made himself a novice of fame. On the contrary, he professed immortality the very first day.

Against the advice of most, he surrounded Cambray, because he was as extravagant in comprehension as in courage. He was known as a hero rather than a soldier.[46]

Much is required to perform with great expectations. Those who watch conceive extravagantly, because it costs them less to imagine the feats than the one who executes them.

An unexpected feat is more spectacular than any genius foreseen from expectation.

A cedar grows at first dawn—more than a hyssop in a whole five years—because robust first fruits promise enormity.

(5) Great are the consequences of a maximum antecedent: where the value of fortune, the greatness of wealth, universal applause, and common grace are declared.

(6) But beginnings are not enough to encourage, because progress tends to grow faint. Nero began with the applause of a phoenix and ended with the scorn of a basilisk.[47]

Disproportionate extremes often declare monstrosity.

---

45 Pedro Henriquez de Acevedo, the Count of Fuentes, was a Spanish statesman and general in the service of King Philip II.

46 A reference to his conquering of the French city of Cambray during the Franco-Spanish war of 1595.

47 In European legends, the basilisk is a legendary reptile reputed to be a serpent king who causes death to anyone who looks into its eyes.

(7) It is as difficult to advance your reputation as it is to gain it. Fame grows old and applause expires as well as everything else; because the laws of time know no exception.

Even the philosophers would have condemned the greatest brilliance, which is the sun, as being old and lacking in brilliance if it were not for nature.

The sun alternates its brightness with different horizons, assorted theaters for its brilliance, so that in one sphere, it deprives, and in the other, it is a novelty, sustaining admiration and desire.

It is, therefore, as much of a trick of the sun as it is of the phoenix, to renew greatness, to renew fame, and to be reborn to applause.

The Caesars returned to their Rome after illustrating to the world their greatness, and each time, they were reborn as monarchs: greater and greater with each new conquest.

The king of metals, passing from one world to another, passes from one extreme of contempt to another of esteem.[48]

The greatest perfection loses esteem when it happens daily, and her constant brilliance turns admiration into anger and appreciation into disgust.

---

48 A reference to gold, which is considered the king of metals because it is very rare, costly, and difficult to find.

-XVII-

Every Gift Without Affectation

(1) Every gift, every enhancement, and every perfection must itself envelope the Hero; but none with affectation.

Affectation is the burden of greatness.

It consists in a silent praise of oneself; and to praise oneself is the most certain revilement.

(2) Perfection must be in oneself; praise must be in others; and it is a deserved punishment that he who imprudently remembers himself be discreetly condemned to oblivion by others.

Esteem is very free: it is not subject to artifice, much less to violence. It yields more readily to an unspoken eloquence of gifts than to faded ostentation.

A little self-esteem prevents much applause from others.

Discernment judges every affected gift as violent rather than natural, as apparent rather than true; and thus, a great drop in reputation is experienced.

All narcissists are fools; but those in love with their intelligence have incurable foolishness, because the ailment lies where the remedy ought to be.

The one who displays his gifts with affectation is an eight-fold fool; but there is someone worse: the one who showers affectations on his imperfections.

And then there are those who, fleeing affectation, are affectatious, because they affect not to affect.

Tiberius was proud of his dissimulation prowess, but he did not know how to dissimulate dissimulation. The greatest art of an art consists in concealing it; and the greatest genius is concealing it with an even greater one.

(3) Twice as great is he who understands all perfections in himself, and none in his estimation. With a generous carelessness, he awakens common attention, and being blind to his own gifts, he makes others *Argos*.[49]

This is worthy of being called a miracle of skill: extravagant paths can lead to greatness, but this one, by doing the opposite, leads to the throne of fame and to the canopy of immortality.

---

49 *Argos* in Spanish refers to a very vigilant person.

-XVIII-

If You Wish to Be Great, You Must Emulate Greatness

(1) For the most part, most Heroes lacked sons, let alone Heroic ones, but not imitators: for it seems that heaven created them to be more of an exemplification of courage than propagators of nature.

(2) It is these eminent men who are animated representations of reputation and from whom the Valiant Hero must take lessons of greatness, repeating their deeds and building on their exploits.

(3) Put yourself in every predicament of the Great Heroes, not so much to imitate as to emulate, not to follow them but to get ahead of them.

(4) Achilles was Alexander's heroic vigil, and sleeping on his tomb awakened in him the emulation of his greatness. He opened his eyes, the attentive Macedon, to mourning and to appreciation alike; and he mourned, not for Achilles' death but for himself, for he had yet to become as great.

The spirit of Alexander then moved and engaged Julius Caesar, and what Achilles was to Alexander, Alexander was to Caesar: he inspired him in the principle of life—the boldness of the heart—making him greater than himself, bringing his own fame into controversy and Caesar's greatness into comparison; for if Alexander made the East the distinguished theater of his conquests, Caesar made the West his own.

The magnanimous king of Aragón and Naples, Don Alfonso, used to say that, as the clarion solicits the courageous warhorse, the trumpet of Cesarean fame inflames him.

(5) And note how these heroes inherit greatness through emulation, and fame through greatness.

In every occupation, there are those who are seated with greatness and also those who are seated with infamy. Some are miracles of excellence, and others are the antithesis of miracles. Let the discreet man discern between them; but for this ability, he must have well reviewed the catalog of Heroes in the annals of fame.

Plutarch wrote the syllabus on these retired Heroes in his *Parallels*;[50] and, for modernity, Paolo Giovio did in his *Eulogies*.[51]

Yet the lack of knowledge pertaining to them is a full-blown crisis, which is to be expected; but what ingenuity will show them off?[52] It is easy to assign these Heroes a place in time, but difficult to appreciate them.

----
50 Plutarch was a Greek philosopher, biographer, and historian. He is most famous for his work titled *Parallel Lives*, a series of 48 biographies of famous men.
51 Paolo Giovio was an Italian physician, historian, biographer, and bishop. He is most famous for his work titled *Elogia virorum bellica virtute illustrum* (*Praise of Men Illustrious for Courage in War*).
52 Despite his genius, brilliant writing style, and articulation with the pen, Father Gracián displays his modesty here. He questions if there is an ingenious writer who will teach us about these great Heroes, failing to realize that he is that ingenious writer who is already doing so.

(6) He would be a universal idea, if he did not pass as a miracle, leaving idle all imitation and occupying all admiration, the monarch of Heroes, the first animated wonder of the globe: King Phillip the Fourth of Spain; to that sun of Austria was owed the fourth sphere.[53]

Let him be the universal mirror who reflects everything maximum and great.

Let him be called the Valiant Hero, whom all Heroes desire to emulate, who is the center of all their exploits; and let him be called the epitome of blazons with eminent plurality: the fortunate, for his happiness; the courageous, for his courage; the discreet, for his wit; the most catholic, for his piety; the natural, for his gracefulness; and the universal, for everything.

---

53 "Sun of Austria" refers metaphorically to King Philip's reach and brilliance and literally to his mother, Margaret of Austria, while "the fourth sphere" is taken from *Paradiso*, the third and final part of Dante's *Divine Comedy*, following *Inferno* and *Purgatorio*. In it, Dante mentions the nine spheres of heaven, the fourth of which is the sun, holding all wisdom. Within the sun, which is the earth's source of illumination, Dante meets the greatest examples of prudence: the souls of the wise, who help to illuminate the world intellectually. Here, Gracián is telling us that the fourth sphere is owed to King Philip because of his wisdom and prudence.

-XIX-
A Critical Paradox

(1) To the Valiant Hero, the sting of criticism in Spain is just as dangerous as the ostracism of Athens.[54]

Critics would banish him—if they could—but the districts of fame and the confines of immortality render them impotent.

Paradoxically, there is condemnation for those who sin by not sinning. So it is of critical importance to commit a forgivable mistake in wit or valor, to bring out their envy and quiet their malevolence.

(2) They (envy and malevolence) are impossible to escape, even if you are a Hero of giant splendor, because they are such harpies[55] that, when they do not find a vile prey, they dare to attack the greatest.

There are people whose intentions are a metaphysical poison, who know how to subtly transform gifts, malign

---

54 In ancient Athens, ostracism was the process by which any citizen, including political leaders, could be expelled from the city-state for ten years.

55 A harpy is a rapacious monster described as having the head and body of a woman and the wings and claws of a bird. It is usually depicted as a bird of prey with a woman's face.

perfections, and give a sinister interpretation of even the most justified endeavor.

(3) It is, therefore, a great political trick to allow some pardonable slip, which gnaws envy and distracts the poison of your adversary.

Allow prudence to immunize you with this political strategy; for, being born of venom, it becomes the antidote. By exposing itself to murmuring, it attracts the poison away from the heart.

Besides, the mischief of nature is often the crown of perfection. A mole is known to be an enhancement of beauty.

There are defects without defect. Alcibiades embraced his with courage;[56] Ovid, with ingenuity, calling them the sources of health.[57]

(4) Here, to me, affirming them seems of the highest importance, guiding you towards self-confidence rather than the culture of discretion.

What is the sun without eclipses, the diamond without a cloud, or the queen of the flowers without thorns?

(5) There is no necessity for art where nature is enough. There is no need for affectation where carelessness is sufficient.

---

[56] Alcibiades was an Athenian statesman and general who played a major role in the second half of the Peloponnesian War as a strategic advisor, military commander, and politician. Here, Gracián is referencing his lisp, which he courageously embraced and used to make his speeches even more persuasive and full of charm. Plutarch, the philosopher, asserts that Alcibiades was a most able speaker in addition to his other gifts.

[57] Ovid was a Roman poet whose work was much imitated during the Middle Ages and greatly influenced Western art and literature.

-XX-

The Greatest Crown Jewel and the Phoenix of a Hero's Gifts

(1) All lucidity descends from the Most High, from the Heavenly Father to his children. Virtue is the daughter of his light, with the inheritance of his splendor. But sin is a monster aborted by blindness, whose inheritance is complete and total darkness.

Every Hero has only as much happiness and greatness as he does virtue, for they run parallel from birth to death.

In Saul, virtue was eclipsed by sin, but in David, happiness and greatness were equal.

(2) Constantine[58] was the first among the Caesars to be called *El Magno*,[59] and he was also the first Christian emperor: a superior oracle that, with Christianity, was born twinned with greatness.

---

58 Constantine I, also known as Constantine the Great.
59 *El Magno* is a very emphatic way of calling someone "the Great" in Spanish.

Louis,[60] the most glorious monarch, was the crowned flower in the garden of saints and kings.

Charles,[61] the first emperor of France, achieved the same renown and aspired to that of a saint.

In Spain, the pious King Fernando,[62] commonly called the Saint of Castilla, was the greatest in the world.

---

60   A reference to Saint Louis IX of France, who is remembered for his many crusades against the enemies of Christianity as well as for his reforms to the French legal system and his promotion of Catholicism. His kingdom was considered the greatest in Europe both politically and economically and he was regarded as *primus inter pares,* "first among equals," by the kings of Europe. The ideal Christian king, and an extremely devout Catholic, he is celebrated as the quintessential Christian monarch.

61   A reference to Charlemagne, the Holy Roman Emperor, who is considered the father of modern Europe.

62   Saint Fernando III, King of Castilla and Leon, of a noble heart and forbearing nature, was one of history's most gifted and formidable warriors. He had the soul of a knight dedicated entirely to God and the royal authority to marshal the might of an entire nation against the enemies of Christ. Of holy intentions, all of Saint Fernando's ventures were met with success; he was absolutely invincible—privately, publicly, and in battle. Convinced that there was no holier enterprise than to do one's duty before Christ and that his first obligation was to rescue his own country from the grips of Islam, he conquered more Islamic territory during his reign than any other Spanish king, expelling the Muslims from most of Spain and turning their remaining kings into his obedient vassals. He inflicted on Islam its greatest defeats up until that time, taking possession of Jaen, Córdoba, Seville, Écija, Estepa, and Murcia, restoring all of them to the Christian religion and to Spain and reducing Islamic influence in Andalusia.

(3) The Conqueror, King Jaime I of Aragón,[63] consecrated as many temples to Christ as he conquered battlements.

(4) The two Catholic Monarchs, Fernando and Isabella,[64] were the *ne plus ultra*; I say, they were columns of faith.

Good, chaste, pious, and zealous is the Spanish Philip IV, who, not losing an inch of land, won heaven by force,[65] and he truly conquered more monsters with his virtue than Hercules with his club.

---

63   King Jaime I, also known as Jaime the Conqueror, is the greatest and most renowned of the medieval kings of Aragón, whose early life served as a hard school for the forging of his character. Fearless even as a youth, he once fought an Aragonese noble in hand-to-hand combat, took part in the siege of Castejón, and successfully waged the second war of reconquest in the Kingdom of Valencia. He recounted being wounded in battle in his autobiography, *Llibre dels fets (Book of Deeds)*: "I removed the arrow, and blood came out, rushing down my face. I wiped it off with a cloth and went away laughing, because I did not want my soldiers to be alarmed or lose confidence." In 1856, King Jamie's mummified body was exhumed when the monastery he was buried in underwent repair. A photograph that was taken of the king's face showed the wound above his left eyebrow that he mentioned in his book. His reign of 62 years is not only the longest of any Spanish monarch, but one of the longest monarchical reigns in history.

64   See Father Gracián's second treatise, *El Politico: The Perfect King (1640)*.

65   A master of theology, Father Gracián is referencing Matthew 11:12, which says, "The kingdom of heaven has suffered violence, and the violent take it by force." This means that the kingdom of God presses ahead relentlessly and only the relentless press their way into it.

Among captains, Godfrey de Bouillon,[66] Jorge Kastriota,[67] Rodrigo Díaz de Vivar,[68] the great Gonzalo Fernández de Córdoba,[69] and the astonishment of the Turks, the most serene lord, Don Juan of Austria,[70] who was a mirror of virtue and a temple of Christian piety.

Among the sacrosanct heroes, the first two to whom greatness gave renown were Gregory and Leo,[71] who achieved splendor through sanctity.

(5) Even among the infidels, the sun of genius, Augustus,[72] used his greatness to form the foundation of some moral virtues.

---

66 Godfrey of Bouillon was a preeminent leader of the First Crusade and the first ruler of the Kingdom of Jerusalem.

67 Gjergj Kastrioti, commonly known as Skanderbeg, was an Albanian feudal lord and military commander who led a rebellion against the Ottoman Empire. He ranks in the military history of that time as the most persistent—and victorious—opponent of the Ottoman Empire. Still today, he is honored in modern Albania and is commemorated with many monuments and cultural works.

68 Rodrigo Diaz de Vivar, known as "El Cid" (the Lord and Master), was a Castilian mercenary, knight, devoted husband, father, and ruler of the kingdom of Valencia. Considered the greatest of all medieval knights, he was undefeated in battle and is still today Spain's celebrated national hero, representing the ideal masculine man: strong, valiant, loyal, just, and pious.

69 Gonzalo Fernández de Córdoba, nicknamed "El Gran Capitán" (The Great Captain), was a Spanish General famous for his exploits during the Italian Wars. He is written about in detail in the third chapter of Gracián's *El Discreto: The Complete Man (1646)*.

70 Don Juan of Austria was a military leader best known for his role as the admiral of the Holy League Fleet at the Battle of Lepanto, where the Holy Pontiff, Pope Pius V, and the Empire of Spain, under King Philip II, inflicted a major defeat on the Ottoman Empire.

71 A reference to Pope Gregory I, commonly known as Saint Gregory the Great, and Pope Leo I, also known as Saint Leo the Great.

72 Gaius Julius Caesar Augustus, the founder of the Roman Empire.

Alexander[73] grew until his morals waned. Hercules overcame monsters of might until he surrendered to the strength of the cloak.[74]

(6) Fortune was as cruel, but I say just, to Emperor Nero as he was to his vassals.[75]

Monsters of lewdness and laziness were Sardanapalus,[76] Caligula,[77] and Rodrigo,[78] and portents of punishment also.

(7) The monarchies of history profess evidence of this primary instruction. Kingdoms thrived while piety and religion flourished, but they withered away their beauty with heresy.

---

73 A reference to Alexander the Great.

74 A reference to Hercules and the poisoned cloak that burned him and caused excruciating pain.

75 Emperor Nero is remembered as a monster and sadist with a chilling list of crimes to his name, from burning down his own capital city to sleeping with his mother and murdering many of his close relatives. When he was declared a public enemy by the Roman senator Vindex with support from the eventual Roman emperor Galba, he fled Rome, and on June 9, AD 68, he committed suicide.

76 Sardanapalus, King of Assyria, lived in the 7th century BC. He was a decadent figure who spent his life in self-indulgence and died in an orgy of destruction. He exceeded all previous rulers in sloth and luxury, dressing in women's clothes, wearing makeup, and staffing many concubines, female and male. He also wrote his own epitaph, which stated that physical gratification was the only purpose of life.

77 Caligula was barbarously cruel, delighting in torture and bloodshed. Among the many horrible things Caligula did, he sexually defiled two of his own sisters, and also insisted on divine honors being paid to him as a god.

78 Rodrigo was the last king of the Visigoths in Northern Spain (later called the Kingdom of Asturias). Here, Gracián alludes to his rape of a young girl.

The phoenix of the provinces perished in the fire of Rodrigo and was reborn in the piety of Pelayo[79] and in the zeal of Fernando the Catholic.

The most august House of Austria became a marvel of ancestry, founding his greatness in piety and becoming one of the marvels of God. And he signed his imperial blood with that of Christ, our Lord, becoming sacramentalized.[80]

(8) Oh, then, learned man, emulator of Heroism! Note this most important and primary instruction, and commit to it with the most constant dexterity.

Greatness cannot be founded in sin, which is hideous, but in Christ, who is everything.

If secular excellence consists of greed, then eternal excellence consists of ambition.

To be a hero of the world is worthless; but to be a Hero of Heaven is everything. To our great Savior and Monarch, our King and Lord, be all the praise, honor, and glory. Amen.

---

79 "The phoenix of the provinces" refers to the Kingdom of Asturias in Northern Spain; "perished in the fire of Rodrigo" refers to Rodrigo's defeat in the Battle of Guadalete; and Pelayo was the Hispano-Visigoth nobleman who founded the Christian Kingdom of Asturias afterwards. He is credited with initiating the Christian reconquest of Spain from Islam and establishing the Asturian monarchy, making him the forefather of all the future Spanish monarchs, including the Kings of Castilla, the Kings of León, and the Kings of Portugal.

80 A reference to the Holy Roman Emperor Charles V of the House of Habsburg, also known as the House of Austria.

Works by Baltasar Gracián

El Héroe (1637)

El Político (1640)

El Arte de Ingenio (1642)

El Discreto (1646)

El Oráculo Manual y Arte de Prudencia (1647)

El Comulgatorio (1655)

El Criticón (1651–1657)

About the Translator

Website: https://StVitus.Dance
Email: TheMikeSanPedro@gmail.com

www.ingramcontent.com/pod-product-compliance
Lightning Source LLC
LaVergne TN
LVHW050840080526
838202LV00029B/2637/J